SEBASTIAN HART

METAVERSE

A Guide to Virtual World and Beyond

First edition

This book was professionally typeset on Reedsy.
Find out more at reedsy.com

"The future belongs to those who can imagine it, design it, and execute it."
— Mohammed bin Rashid Al Maktoum
"We are limited not by our technology, but by our imagination."
— John C. Maxwell
As we step into the Metaverse, we are not just entering a new digital era—we are creating a new reality. The question is: Will we shape it, or will it shape us?

SEBASTIAN HART

Contents

Preface   ii

Acknowledgments   xiv

1   The Dawn of the Metaverse   1

2   The Technology Behind the Metaverse   5

3   How the Metaverse Works   13

4   Virtual Worlds & Platforms in the Metaverse   21

5   Metaverse Applications in Business, Education, and...   29

6   Social Interaction, Entertainment, and Culture in the...   38

7   The Economy of the Metaverse – Digital Assets,...   47

8   The Ethical and Legal Implications of the Metaverse   86

9   The Future of the Metaverse – Opportunities and Challenges   121

10   Conclusion and Final Thoughts   163

11   References   227

Preface

Preface

The Metaverse is no longer a concept confined to science fiction or the imaginations of tech enthusiasts. It is becoming a reality—an evolving digital landscape that promises to transform how we live, work, interact, and experience the world around us. From virtual reality (VR) to blockchain-powered economies, from digital identities to decentralized governance, the Metaverse represents a **paradigm shift in human interaction**. But with this transformation comes a host of challenges, ethical dilemmas, and opportunities that demand our attention.

This book is an exploration of the **past, present, and future of the Metaverse**. It is not just a technological deep dive but also a reflection on its **social, economic, and cultural implications**. As we stand on the brink of this digital revolution, it is crucial to understand not just **what the Metaverse is** but also **what it could become**. Will it be an inclusive space that democratizes digital experiences, or will it fall into the hands of monopolistic corporations, exacerbating social inequalities? Will it enhance human creativity and connection, or will it push society further into digital isolation? These are the questions that this book seeks to explore.

Why This Book?

The idea of writing this book emerged from a realization: while the Metaverse is frequently discussed in news articles, social media, and tech conferences, there is **a lack of comprehensive yet accessible resources** that explore its **technological, philosophical, and societal dimensions** in an integrated manner. Many existing discussions focus on one aspect—whether it be **VR advancements, cryptocurrency markets, or gaming ecosystems**—but few attempt to connect these elements into a **cohesive narrative**.

This book is designed to fill that gap by offering a **balanced, well-researched, and easy-to-understand** exploration of the Metaverse. It is written for:

Tech Enthusiasts & Developers – Those interested in understanding how the Metaverse is built, what technologies power it, and where it is headed.

Entrepreneurs & Business Leaders – Individuals looking to explore **Metaverse-based business opportunities, virtual economies, and the future of digital commerce**.

Students & Researchers – Readers who want an in-depth yet accessible resource to guide them through **Metaverse-related academic
discussions, policy implications, and future research areas**.

General Readers Curious About the Future – Anyone fascinated by how digital worlds could **reshape our lives, jobs, relationships, and cultural norms**.

By the end of this book, my hope is that you will have gained not just **technical knowledge about the Metaverse**, but also a **critical perspective** on its ethical, social, and economic implications.

The Structure of This Book

To provide a comprehensive and structured understanding of the Metaverse, this book is divided into ten chapters, each exploring a different aspect:

1. **Understanding the Metaverse** – A foundational introduction that explains **what the Metaverse is, its historical evolution, and its core technologies.**
2. **The Technologies Powering the Metaverse** – A deep dive into **VR, AR, blockchain, AI, and cloud computing**, which serve as the Metaverse's backbone.
3. **The Metaverse Economy** – An exploration of **virtual real estate, cryptocurrency, NFTs, and digital job markets**.
4. **Social and Psychological Impacts** – A look at how the Metaverse affects **identity, human connection, mental health, and digital culture**.
5. **Education and Learning in the Metaverse** – How immersive learning environments are transforming **education, training, and skill development**.
6. **The Future of Work in the Metaverse** – How businesses, organizations, and remote workforces will function in **Metaverse-based offices and decentralized workspaces**.
7. **Governance, Privacy, and Security** – A discussion on the **legal and ethical challenges** associated with virtual worlds.
8. **Metaverse and Ethics: The Big Questions** – Analyzing the risks of **digital inequality, AI-driven surveillance, and ethical dilemmas** in Metaverse development.
9. **The Future of the Metaverse** – Predictions and potential outcomes, from **utopian digital societies to dystopian surveillance states**.

10. **Conclusion and Final Thoughts** – A summary of key insights, a call to action, and reflections on the path forward.

Each chapter is structured to **balance technical depth with readability**, making complex topics **accessible to a wide audience**. Whether you are new to the concept of the Metaverse or already well-versed in its development, this book is designed to **offer new perspectives, insights, and practical takeaways**.

The Ethical Imperative

One of the recurring themes throughout this book is **the ethical responsibility that comes with shaping the Metaverse**. Unlike the early days of the internet, where regulatory frameworks were developed retrospectively, we have the **unique opportunity to design the Metaverse with ethics, inclusivity, and sustainability in mind from the start**.

Who will control the Metaverse?   Will it be owned by a few corporations, or will it be a decentralized, user-driven ecosystem?

How do we ensure digital rights and privacy? As immersive platforms collect vast amounts of personal data, how can we **protect user autonomy**?

What happens to digital labor and economies? As people begin to work and earn in virtual worlds, how do we **prevent economic exploitation**?

Will the Metaverse be accessible to all? How do we ensure that the Metaverse does not become an **exclusive playground for the privileged few** while leaving others behind?

By addressing these questions, we can shape a **Metaverse that is fair, inclusive, and empowering rather than exploitative**.

Acknowledgments

This book would not have been possible without the **contributions, insights, and inspiration** provided by researchers, developers, and thought leaders in the field. I am grateful to the countless innovators who are pushing the boundaries of **virtual reality, blockchain, AI, and immersive experiences**, as well as the philosophers and ethicists who remind us of our **social responsibility** in designing these technologies.

I also extend my gratitude to the readers—whether you are a **tech visionary, an entrepreneur, a student, or simply someone curious about the future**—for taking the time to explore this complex yet fascinating topic. The Metaverse is still **in its infancy**, and its direction will be shaped by **people like you** who choose to engage with it critically and constructively.

1

The Dawn of the Metaverse

1.1 INTRODUCTION

The term "Metaverse" has become one of the most discussed concepts in technology and digital innovation. It represents a virtual, immersive world where users interact, socialize, and engage in various activities through digital avatars. Although the idea gained mainstream attention in recent years, its origins trace back to science fiction and early internet developments. This chapter explores the history, evolution, and foundational concepts of the Metaverse, providing a clear understanding of how it came to be.

1.2 The Origin of the Term "Metaverse"

The word "Metaverse" was first introduced in 1992 by American author **Neal Stephenson** in his novel *Snow Crash*. In this cyberpunk novel, the Metaverse was depicted as a vast virtual reality space where individuals, through avatars, could interact, conduct business, and escape from the dystopian real world. This fictional portrayal laid the foundation for what later evolved into the real-world concept of the Metaverse.

Beyond Stephenson's work, the idea of immersive digital worlds has been a recurring theme in literature and media. **Ernest Cline's** *Ready Player One* (2011) further popularized the notion of a persistent, interactive, and economically viable virtual universe, reinforcing the possibilities of a digital society beyond physical limitations.

1.3 Early Digital Worlds and Virtual Environments

The development of virtual worlds began long before the term "Metaverse" was coined. Some of the earliest examples include:

1. **MUDs (Multi-User Dungeons) – 1970s-1980s:** These were text-based online environments where players could explore, interact, and complete quests collaboratively. While simple, they marked the beginning of shared virtual spaces.
2. **Massively Multiplayer Online Games (MMORPGs) – 1990s:** Games like *Ultima Online* (1997) and *EverQuest* (1999) introduced graphical multiplayer worlds where players could create avatars, interact with others, and participate in virtual economies.
3. **Second Life (2003):** Often considered a precursor to the modern Metaverse, *Second Life* provided an open-world platform where users could create digital identities, own virtual property, and engage in real-world economic transactions.

These early platforms demonstrated the potential for fully immersive digital environments, setting the stage for more advanced iterations of the Metaverse.

1.4 The Evolution of Virtual Reality and Augmented Reality

The Metaverse concept relies heavily on advancements in **Virtual**

Reality (VR) and Augmented Reality (AR) technologies. These innovations have gradually evolved to provide more immersive and interactive digital experiences:

- **Early VR Experiments (1960s-1980s):** The first VR headsets, such as the "Sword of Damocles" (1968) by Ivan Sutherland, introduced the concept of immersive virtual displays. However, due to technological limitations, widespread adoption was not feasible.
- **Gaming and Commercial VR (1990s-2000s):** Devices like the Nintendo Virtual Boy (1995) and early PC-based VR systems attempted to bring VR to consumers but faced issues with affordability and performance.
- **Modern VR & AR (2010s-Present):** The release of the **Oculus Rift (2016), HTC Vive, PlayStation VR, and Meta's Quest series** significantly advanced VR adoption. Similarly, AR technologies like **Microsoft HoloLens and Pokémon GO** demonstrated the potential of blending virtual and physical experiences.

These technological breakthroughs are shaping the infrastructure necessary for a fully realized Metaverse.

1.5 The Role of Blockchain and Web3 in the Metaverse

The Metaverse is not just about immersive digital environments— it also incorporates decentralized technologies like **blockchain** and **Web3** to create digital ownership, secure transactions, and decentralized governance.

- **Blockchain & Digital Ownership:** Non-Fungible Tokens (NFTs) allow users to own unique digital assets, such as virtual land, avatars, and collectibles.

- **Cryptocurrency & Virtual Economies:** Many Metaverse platforms operate on digital currencies, enabling real-world value exchange within virtual spaces.
- **Decentralized Autonomous Organizations (DAOs):** These community-driven governance structures allow users to influence the development and rules of virtual spaces.

The integration of these technologies ensures that the Metaverse is not controlled by a single entity, promoting decentralization and user-driven innovation.

1.6 Conclusion

The Metaverse is not a sudden innovation but a concept that has gradually evolved through literature, gaming, virtual reality, and blockchain technology. While still in its early stages, the Metaverse holds the potential to revolutionize how we interact, work, and live in digital spaces. As we explore its various components in subsequent chapters, it becomes clear that the Metaverse is more than just a trend— it represents a fundamental shift in the digital world.

2

The Technology Behind the Metaverse

2.1 Introduction

The Metaverse is not just a virtual world; it is an ecosystem built on advanced digital technologies that enable seamless interaction, immersion, and decentralized ownership. From **virtual reality (VR) and augmented reality (AR)** to **blockchain, artificial intelligence (AI), cloud computing, and 5G,** multiple technological innovations converge to create the infrastructure of the Metaverse. This chapter explores the key technologies that power the Metaverse, their functions, and their impact on the future of digital experiences.

2.2 Virtual Reality (VR) and Augmented Reality (AR)

The foundation of the Metaverse lies in **immersive digital experiences**, which are made possible by VR and AR. These technologies allow users to engage with virtual environments in an interactive and realistic manner.

2.2.1 Virtual Reality (VR)

Virtual Reality creates fully immersive digital worlds that users can explore through VR headsets. These devices track head movements and provide stereoscopic 3D visuals, enhancing depth perception and spatial awareness.

Key Components of VR Technology:

- **VR Headsets:** Devices such as **Meta Quest, HTC Vive, and PlayStation VR** offer users entry into digital spaces.
- **Haptic Feedback:** Special gloves and suits enhance the experience by simulating touch sensations.
- **Motion Tracking:** Sensors track body and hand movements to allow natural interactions.

VR in the Metaverse:

- Social platforms like **Horizon Worlds and VRChat** allow users to interact in shared virtual environments.
- Virtual workspaces such as **Meta's Workrooms** enable remote collaboration in immersive 3D offices.

2.2.2 Augmented Reality (AR)

Unlike VR, **Augmented Reality** overlays digital elements onto the real world using devices such as smartphones, tablets, and AR glasses.

AR Technologies in the Metaverse:

- **AR Smart Glasses** (e.g., Microsoft HoloLens, Apple Vision Pro) merge virtual elements with the physical world.
- **AR Applications** enhance real-world experiences, such as **Poké-**

mon GO blending digital creatures into real environments.
- **Retail & Fashion:** AR enables virtual try-ons for clothes, furniture, and makeup.

With continuous improvements in **wearable AR devices**, the future Metaverse will likely integrate the real and virtual worlds seamlessly.

2.3 Blockchain and Decentralization

The Metaverse is not just about virtual experiences—it also relies on blockchain technology to enable **digital ownership, security, and decentralized control**.

2.3.1 Digital Ownership with NFTs

Non-Fungible Tokens (**NFTs**) represent unique digital assets that users can own, trade, and sell within the Metaverse. Examples include:

- **Virtual Real Estate:** Platforms like **Decentraland and The Sandbox** allow users to buy virtual land as NFTs.
- **Digital Avatars & Skins:** Users can personalize their avatars with exclusive outfits and accessories.
- **Collectibles & Art:** NFT-based digital art and in-game items hold real-world value.

2.3.2 Cryptocurrency and Virtual Economies

Most Metaverse platforms operate on **cryptocurrencies** rather than traditional money. Some key examples:

- **Ethereum (ETH):** A widely used blockchain supporting Metaverse projects.
- **MANA (Decentraland) & SAND (The Sandbox):** Native tokens for purchasing land and services.
- **Bitcoin & Stablecoins:** Used for transactions and maintaining value stability.

Cryptocurrencies ensure **secure, transparent, and decentralized transactions** within the Metaverse, reducing reliance on centralized financial systems.

2.3.3 Smart Contracts & DAOs

- **Smart Contracts:** Self-executing contracts on blockchains automate agreements in the Metaverse (e.g., virtual land sales, digital art transfers).
- **Decentralized Autonomous Organizations (DAOs):** User-led governance structures that empower communities to make decisions about Metaverse platforms.

Blockchain technology guarantees **trust, security, and decentralization**, making the Metaverse **user-driven rather than corporate-controlled**.

2.4 Artificial Intelligence (AI) in the Metaverse

AI plays a crucial role in **enhancing experiences, generating content, and automating interactions** within the Metaverse.

2.4.1 AI-Generated Avatars & NPCs

- **Personalized Avatars:** AI creates lifelike avatars by scanning facial features and movements.
- **Non-Player Characters (NPCs):** AI-driven virtual beings provide real-time interactions in Metaverse spaces.

2.4.2 AI-Powered Content Creation

AI assists in generating digital environments, 3D objects, and even virtual landscapes through machine learning. **Example:** AI-powered game engines like **Unreal Engine 5** create realistic virtual spaces.

2.4.3 AI Chatbots and Virtual Assistants

- **AI-powered chatbots** offer customer support in virtual stores.
- **AI Assistants (like ChatGPT)** help guide users in Metaverse spaces.

By **automating tasks and improving realism**, AI makes the Metaverse more immersive and efficient.

2.5 Cloud Computing and Edge Computing

The Metaverse requires massive processing power and real-time rendering, which is supported by **cloud computing** and **edge computing**.

2.5.1 Cloud Computing

Cloud services such as **Microsoft Azure, AWS, and Google Cloud** provide scalable infrastructure for running Metaverse platforms.

- **On-demand storage & computing** allows for high-quality virtual

experiences without requiring high-end devices.
- **Cross-platform accessibility** enables users to access the Metaverse on various devices.

2.5.2 Edge Computing

Edge computing processes data **closer to the user**, reducing latency and improving real-time interactions.

- **Example:** 5G-powered edge servers allow instant rendering of virtual environments without delays.
- **Impact: Low-latency gaming, seamless VR streaming, and real-time social interactions.**

Cloud and edge computing ensure **smooth, high-performance Metaverse experiences**, even on lower-end devices.

2.6 5G & Internet Infrastructure

A fast, reliable internet connection is crucial for the Metaverse. **5G technology** enables **low latency, high-speed data transfer, and uninterrupted connectivity.**

2.6.1 The Role of 5G in the Metaverse

- **Faster Speeds:** 5G enables **instant rendering** of complex 3D environments.
- **Lower Latency:** Reduces lag in VR and AR interactions, making them more **realistic and responsive**.
- **Seamless Streaming:** Supports **cloud-based VR gaming** and live-streamed events.

As **6G and satellite-based internet** (e.g., Starlink) develop, global Metaverse access will expand, enabling broader participation.

2.7 Cybersecurity and Privacy in the Metaverse

With an increasing number of users engaging in virtual worlds, security and privacy concerns arise.

2.7.1 Data Security Challenges

- **User Identity Theft:** Digital avatars can be hacked or misused.
- **Phishing & Scams:** Fraudsters exploit virtual transactions.

2.7.2 Privacy Concerns

- **Personal Data Tracking:** Companies collect vast amounts of behavioral data.
- **Facial Recognition & Biometric Data Risks:** Some VR devices track **eye movements and body gestures**, raising privacy concerns.

Solutions such as **decentralized identity systems, biometric encryption, and blockchain verification** are being explored to improve cybersecurity in the Metaverse.

2.8 Conclusion

The Metaverse is built on a **complex technological ecosystem**, combining **VR/AR, blockchain, AI, cloud computing, 5G, and cybersecurity**. Each of these components plays a crucial role in **creating, maintaining, and securing** immersive virtual environments. As these technologies evolve, they will shape the Metaverse into a **more scalable, decentralized, and interactive** digital world.

In the next chapter, we will explore **how the Metaverse functions,** focusing on **decentralization, digital identities, virtual economies, and interoperability**.

3

How the Metaverse Works

3.1 Introduction

The Metaverse is more than just a collection of virtual worlds—it is a **complex, interconnected ecosystem** that integrates **decentralization, digital identities, virtual economies, and interoperability**. Unlike traditional online platforms, where users are limited to closed environments, the Metaverse enables **seamless interaction, ownership, and movement** across different virtual spaces. This chapter explores how the Metaverse operates, covering its core principles, infrastructure, and the technologies that make it function.

3.2 Decentralization: The Backbone of the Metaverse

Traditional online platforms, such as social media and gaming worlds, are controlled by centralized entities like **Meta (Facebook), Google, and Microsoft**. In contrast, the Metaverse is envisioned as a **decen-**

tralized space, meaning no single corporation or government has complete control over it.

3.2.1 What is Decentralization in the Metaverse?

Decentralization means that virtual spaces, economies, and governance structures are **distributed** across multiple servers and networks rather than being owned by a single entity. This is achieved through **blockchain technology, peer-to-peer networks, and decentralized governance models (DAOs).**

3.2.2 Key Aspects of Decentralization

- **Blockchain-Based Ownership:** Users can truly own digital assets, such as avatars, virtual land, and in-game items, through **NFTs (Non-Fungible Tokens).**
- **Decentralized Autonomous Organizations (DAOs):** Communities within the Metaverse can govern themselves without centralized authority. DAOs allow users to vote on platform decisions, policies, and updates.
- **Peer-to-Peer Transactions:** Unlike traditional platforms that rely on payment processors (Visa, PayPal), the Metaverse uses **cryptocurrencies** for transactions, eliminating intermediaries.

Example:

- **Decentraland** is a fully decentralized Metaverse platform where users own and trade virtual land through blockchain-based smart contracts. Unlike **Meta's Horizon Worlds**, which is controlled by a single company, Decentraland is governed by its users via a DAO.

3.3 Digital Identities in the Metaverse

In the Metaverse, users interact through **digital identities**, which include **avatars, profiles, and blockchain-based credentials.** Unlike social media, where identities are tied to real-world names, Metaverse identities offer anonymity, customization, and persistence across platforms.

3.3.1 Avatars: The Digital Representation of Users

Avatars are **3D digital representations** that users create to navigate virtual environments. These avatars can be simple cartoonish characters or hyper-realistic models.

Types of Avatars:

- **Static Avatars:** Used in games like *Roblox* and *The Sandbox*.
- **Animated Avatars:** Full-body avatars with motion-tracking capabilities in VR environments (e.g., *Horizon Worlds, VRChat*).
- **AI-Generated Avatars:** AI-enhanced avatars that mimic real-world facial expressions and body movements.

3.3.2 Decentralized Identity (DID) and Security

Traditional online identities rely on usernames and passwords, making them vulnerable to hacking. In the Metaverse, **Decentralized Identity (DID)** systems use blockchain-based verification to ensure security and user control.

How DID Works:

- Users create a **self-sovereign identity (SSI)** that stores their credentials securely on a blockchain.
- Verification is done through cryptographic keys, eliminating the need for passwords.
- Personal data remains **private** and is only shared when users permit it.

Example:

- Projects like **ENS (Ethereum Name Service)** allow users to own human-readable blockchain-based usernames (e.g., *yourname.eth*), serving as their digital identity in the Metaverse.

3.4 Virtual Economies and Digital Assets

The Metaverse features **fully functional economies**, where users can earn, spend, and trade digital assets. Unlike traditional gaming economies, where virtual items are owned by game developers, the Metaverse enables users to have **true ownership** through blockchain technology.

3.4.1 Digital Currencies and Cryptocurrencies

Transactions in the Metaverse are conducted using cryptocurrencies rather than traditional fiat money.

Common Metaverse Cryptocurrencies:

- **MANA (Decentraland):** Used for purchasing virtual land and in-game goods.

- **SAND (The Sandbox):** Powers The Sandbox economy, enabling users to buy, sell, and create experiences.
- **ETH (Ethereum):** Widely used for NFT transactions in various Metaverse platforms.

3.4.2 Virtual Land and Real Estate

Virtual land is one of the most valuable assets in the Metaverse. Users can **buy, sell, lease, and develop** digital real estate using blockchain-based NFTs.

How Virtual Real Estate Works:

- Land is represented as **NFTs** on the blockchain.
- Owners can build **businesses, events, or experiences** on their land.
- Virtual property values **appreciate** based on location, demand, and development.

Example:

- In **Decentraland**, companies like **Samsung and JPMorgan** have purchased virtual real estate to establish a presence in the Metaverse.

3.4.3 Play-to-Earn (P2E) and Work Opportunities

Unlike traditional gaming, where players spend money, **Play-to-Earn (P2E)** models allow users to **earn cryptocurrency** by engaging in Metaverse activities.

Examples of P2E Models:

- **Axie Infinity:** Players earn cryptocurrency by breeding and battling digital pets.
- **The Sandbox:** Users monetize virtual land by creating experiences.
- **Metaverse Freelancing:** Users can offer virtual services like fashion design for avatars, event hosting, and NFT art creation.

3.5 Interoperability: Connecting Virtual Worlds

One of the biggest challenges of the Metaverse is **interoperability**—the ability for users to move their assets, identities, and experiences across different virtual worlds.

3.5.1 Why is Interoperability Important?

Currently, most digital platforms operate as **walled gardens**, meaning assets and identities cannot be transferred across different systems. True interoperability allows:

- **Seamless avatar and asset transfers** across platforms.
- **Cross-platform virtual experiences** (e.g., attending a Decentraland concert with a Sandbox-purchased avatar).
- **Unified economies** where users can spend cryptocurrency across multiple Metaverse spaces.

3.5.2 The Role of Open Standards in the Metaverse

Developers are working on **universal protocols** to ensure different virtual environments can communicate.

Key Technologies Enabling Interoperability:

- **Metaverse Standards Forum:** A coalition of companies (Meta, Microsoft, Nvidia) developing open Metaverse protocols.
- **Open Metaverse Initiative:** Projects like **Web3 ID, VRM avatars, and cross-chain compatibility** are being developed to allow interoperability.
- **Layer 2 Solutions:** Blockchain solutions that enable cross-platform asset transfers.

Example:

- A user could buy a **NFT outfit in The Sandbox** and wear it in **Decentraland or Meta's Horizon Worlds** using interoperability standards.

3.6 Challenges and Limitations

While the Metaverse presents enormous potential, it still faces several challenges:

3.6.1 Scalability Issues

- High-quality virtual experiences require massive computing power.
- Solutions: Cloud gaming, edge computing, and AI-based optimization.

3.6.2 Security Risks

- Identity theft, hacking, and scams are major threats.
- Solutions: Decentralized identity systems and enhanced encryption.

3.6.3 Regulation and Legal Concerns

- Governments struggle to regulate **virtual property rights and taxation**.
- Solutions: Standardized legal frameworks for digital ownership and transactions.

3.7 Conclusion

The Metaverse operates on a **decentralized, blockchain-driven infrastructure** that enables **digital identities, virtual economies, and interoperability**. By merging advanced technologies like AI, VR, and Web3, it creates a **seamless and immersive digital world** where users can work, socialize, and earn. However, achieving a **fully connected Metaverse** requires overcoming **interoperability, security, and scalability challenges**.

In the next chapter, we will explore the **various Metaverse platforms** and compare their technologies, economies, and use cases.

4

Virtual Worlds & Platforms in the Metaverse

4.1 Introduction

The Metaverse is not a single platform but a collection of **virtual worlds** that offer unique experiences, from gaming and social interaction to business and education. These platforms vary in terms of **technology, decentralization, user base, and economic models**. Some are built on **blockchain technology**, allowing true digital ownership, while others remain centralized but provide immersive experiences.

This chapter explores the most influential Metaverse platforms, categorizing them into **blockchain-based decentralized worlds and centralized virtual environments**. We will examine their key features, technologies, and real-world applications.

4.2 Categories of Metaverse Platforms

Metaverse platforms can be classified into two major categories:

4.2.1 Decentralized Metaverse Platforms

These platforms operate on **blockchain technology** and enable users to own virtual land, assets, and identities through **NFTs and cryptocurrencies**. Users have control over their digital possessions and can transfer them across platforms.

4.2.2 Centralized Metaverse Platforms

These platforms are controlled by corporations and function as closed ecosystems. While they offer high-quality immersive experiences, users do not have **true ownership** of assets, which remain within the company's control.

4.3 Decentralized Metaverse Platforms

Decentralized Metaverse platforms leverage **blockchain, NFTs, and cryptocurrencies** to enable ownership, governance, and decentralized economies.

4.3.1 Decentraland
Overview:

- One of the most well-known blockchain-based Metaverse platforms.
- Users can buy, sell, and develop virtual land using **MANA cryp-**

tocurrency (Ethereum-based).
- Features virtual businesses, casinos, art galleries, and music concerts.

Key Features:
User-Owned Land: Virtual plots are NFTs that can be traded.

Decentralized Governance: Controlled by a **DAO** where users vote on platform rules.

Real-World Economy: Users earn income through land rentals, event hosting, and
virtual businesses.

Example:

- Companies like **Atari, Samsung, and JPMorgan** have virtual offices in Decentraland.
- **NFT Art Galleries** display and sell digital artwork.

4.3.2 The Sandbox
Overview:

- A blockchain-based virtual world where users create, own, and monetize experiences.
- Uses **SAND cryptocurrency** for transactions.

Key Features:
Voxel-Based World: Similar to Minecraft but with NFT ownership.

Play-to-Earn Model: Users can create mini-games and monetize them.

NFT Market: Users trade avatars, virtual real estate, and in-game assets.

Example:

- **Snoop Dogg's Metaverse Mansion** was built in The Sandbox, with virtual parties and NFT collections.
- **Adidas** created virtual wearables for Sandbox avatars.

4.3.3 Otherside (by Yuga Labs)
Overview:

- A Metaverse project developed by **Yuga Labs**, creators of **Bored Ape Yacht Club (BAYC)** NFTs.
- Integrates NFT collections like **Bored Apes, CryptoPunks, and Meebits** into an interactive world.

Key Features:
NFT Integration: Users play as their NFT characters.
Dynamic Virtual Land: Land NFTs called **Otherdeeds** evolve based on user
interaction.
Interoperability: Future plans include **cross-platform NFT movement**.

4.4 Centralized Metaverse Platforms

Centralized platforms are developed and controlled by corporations. While they offer **better graphics, smoother experiences, and extensive user bases**, they **lack decentralization** and true digital ownership.

4.4.1 Meta's Horizon Worlds
Overview:

- Developed by **Meta (Facebook)**, it is a VR-based social Metaverse.
- Requires **Meta Quest headsets** for full immersion.

Key Features:

3D Virtual Worlds: Users build and explore VR spaces.

Social Interaction: Users engage in virtual events, business meetings, and social

hangouts.

Limited Monetization: Users can sell digital goods but within Meta's controlled

ecosystem.

Example:

- **Meta has invested over $10 billion** into Horizon Worlds.
- **VR concerts, conferences, and educational experiences** are hosted in the platform.

4.4.2 Microsoft Mesh

Overview:

- A professional Metaverse platform focused on **virtual collaboration and business applications**.
- Works with **Microsoft Teams** for enterprise-level meetings.

Key Features:

Holographic Meetings: Users interact via 3D avatars in mixed reality spaces.

Enterprise-Focused: Businesses can conduct **remote training, simulations, and**

meetings.

AI & AR Integration: Uses AI-generated avatars and **HoloLens** AR

technology.
Example:

- **Accenture** uses Microsoft Mesh for **onboarding new employees** in virtual offices.

4.4.3 Roblox
Overview:

- A massively popular online platform where users create and play games.
- Features a digital economy using **Robux currency**.

Key Features:
User-Generated Content: Millions of games and virtual experiences.

Massive User Base: Over **200 million monthly active users**.

Limited Ownership: Users do not truly own in-game items (centralized model).

Example:

- Brands like **Nike, Gucci, and Vans** have created virtual stores in Roblox.
- Roblox hosted a **Lil Nas X virtual concert** attended by millions.

4.5 Virtual Economy Comparison

The virtual economy within the metaverse is a fascinating and evolving concept, blending elements of blockchain technology, digital assets, and user-generated content. Here's a brief comparison of key aspects:

- **Digital Assets and Ownership:** The metaverse economy heavily relies on digital assets like cryptocurrencies and NFTs (Non-Fungible Tokens). These assets enable users to own, trade, and monetize virtual goods, such as virtual land, art, or even avatars.
- **Economic Cycles:** Unlike traditional economies, the metaverse operates on unique cycles, including inner cycles (within the virtual world), outer cycles (interactions with the real world), and virtual-real cycles that bridge both.
- **Decentralization**: Blockchain technology underpins the metaverse economy, ensuring transparency and decentralization. This contrasts with traditional economies, which often rely on centralized institutions.
- **User-Centric Model**: The metaverse thrives on user-generated content, making users both consumers and producers. This participatory model is reshaping economic dynamics.
- **Challenges and Opportunities**: While the metaverse offers immense potential for innovation and creativity, challenges like security, regulation, and scalability remain.

4.6 The Future of Metaverse Platforms

The competition between **centralized vs. decentralized** Metaverse platforms will define the industry's future.

4.6.1 Trends to Watch

Interoperability: Platforms are working on cross-world asset transfers.

VR & AR Advancements: Improved **haptic feedback, AI avatars, and neural interfaces**.

Regulation & Monetization: Governments are exploring **Metaverse taxation and
digital property rights**.

4.6.2 Challenges

Scalability Issues: VR worlds require significant computing power.
Privacy Concerns: Centralized platforms collect vast amounts of personal data.
Economic Risks: NFT markets can be volatile.

4.7 Conclusion

Metaverse platforms vary in terms of **ownership, economy, and purpose**. While **Decentralized platforms** (Decentraland, The Sandbox) offer **true ownership and user governance**, **Centralized platforms** (Meta's Horizon Worlds, Microsoft Mesh) provide **polished, controlled experiences**. The future will likely see **hybrid models**, combining decentralization with **enterprise-grade performance**. In the next chapter, we will explore "**Metaverse Applications in Business, Education, and Healthcare.**"

5

Metaverse Applications in Business, Education, and Healthcare

5.1 Introduction

The Metaverse is no longer just a concept confined to gaming and social interactions—it is rapidly transforming various industries, including **business, education, and healthcare**. With advancements in **VR (Virtual Reality), AR (Augmented Reality), AI (Artificial Intelligence), and blockchain**, organizations are adopting Metaverse technologies to enhance **collaboration, learning, and medical treatments**.

This chapter explores how the Metaverse is revolutionizing **business operations, online education, and digital healthcare**, along with the challenges and future prospects of these applications.

5.2 The Metaverse in Business

The Metaverse is changing the way businesses operate, offering new opportunities for **remote collaboration, marketing, e-commerce, and virtual real estate investment.**

5.2.1 Virtual Offices and Remote Work

With remote work becoming the norm, businesses are shifting from traditional video conferencing tools to **immersive Metaverse workspaces.**

- **Metaverse Meeting Rooms:** Companies use platforms like **Microsoft Mesh, Horizon Workrooms (Meta), and Spatial** to create VR-based virtual offices where employees can interact as avatars.
- **Remote Collaboration:** Employees can **brainstorm, share digital documents, and use 3D visualization tools.**
- **Virtual Co-Working Spaces:** Startups and freelancers can work in **Metaverse**

office spaces, paying rent with cryptocurrency.

Example:

- **Accenture** has built a Metaverse campus called the **Nth Floor**, where it conducts employee training and virtual meetings.

5.2.2 Virtual Commerce and Digital Goods

E-commerce brands are entering the Metaverse to create **immersive** shopping experiences.

- **Virtual Stores & Showrooms:** Brands like **Gucci, Nike, and Samsung** have set up **Metaverse shops** where customers can browse digital products and purchase NFT-based wearables.
- **AI-Powered Shopping Assistants:** AI-driven avatars help users select products and complete transactions in **VR malls**.
- **Cryptocurrency Transactions:** Purchases in Metaverse stores are often made using **crypto wallets and NFTs**.

Example:

- **Nike launched "Nikeland" in Roblox**, where users can buy virtual sneakers for their avatars.

5.2.3 Metaverse Real Estate & Virtual Events

- **Virtual Land Investment:** Investors and companies buy **virtual properties** on platforms like **Decentralized and The Sandbox** to build digital businesses.
- **Virtual Events & Conferences:** Companies host product launches, trade shows, and networking events in the Metaverse.
- **Corporate Training & Simulations:** Businesses use VR simulations for **employee training and skills development**.

Example:

- **JPMorgan** opened a virtual **lounge in Decentraland**, signaling the rise of Metaverse banking.

5.3 The Metaverse in Education

The traditional education system is evolving with **immersive, interactive learning environments** in the Metaverse. Schools and universities are using VR and AR to **enhance engagement, accessibility, and experiential learning**.

5.3.1 Virtual Classrooms and Universities

- **Immersive Lectures:** Professors can teach in **3D classrooms**, making lessons more engaging.
- **Global Access:** Students from different locations can **attend the same virtual university**.
- **AI-Powered Tutors:** AI-driven avatars assist students with real-time queries and interactive lessons.

Example:

- **Stanford University's Virtual Campus:** The university runs courses in VR using **Engage, AltspaceVR, and Mozilla Hubs**.

5.3.2 Interactive Learning Experiences

- **Historical and Science Simulations:** Students can experience **historical events** or conduct **virtual chemistry experiments** in the Metaverse.
- **Gamified Learning:** Platforms like **Minecraft Education Edition** integrate learning with gaming.
- **Language Learning:** AI-driven avatars simulate **real-world conversations** in different languages.

Example:

- **VR History Tours:** Students can walk through **Ancient Rome or the Great Wall of China** in a Metaverse history class.

5.3.3 Corporate Training and Skill Development

Companies use **Metaverse-based training simulations** for skill enhancement.

- **VR Job Training:** Workers practice skills in **realistic digital environments**.
- **Medical Simulations:** Medical students perform **virtual surgeries** before working on real patients.
- **Soft Skill Development:** VR-based training improves **public speaking, teamwork, and leadership**.

Example:

- **Walmart uses VR training for employees** to practice customer service scenarios.

5.4 The Metaverse in Healthcare

The Metaverse is revolutionizing healthcare by offering **virtual medical consultations, AI-assisted diagnostics, and immersive therapy experiences**.

5.4.1 Virtual Medical Consultations & Telemedicine

- **VR-Based Doctor Appointments:** Patients meet doctors in **virtual clinics** instead of

- traditional video calls.
- **AI-Powered Diagnosis:** AI analyzes medical data and **assists doctors in detecting**
- **diseases.**
- **Mental Health Support:** Therapists use **VR therapy** for treating anxiety and PTSD.

Example:

- **XRHealth** provides **VR therapy sessions** for mental health patients.

5.4.2 Medical Training & Surgery Simulations

- **VR Surgery Training:** Surgeons practice **complex procedures in 3D virtual**
- **environments.**
- **Remote-Assisted Surgeries:** Doctors in one country **guide robotic surgeries** in

another via the Metaverse.

- **Anatomy Learning:** Medical students use **VR models of the human body** for

interactive learning.

Example:

- **Johns Hopkins University** successfully conducted a **live surgery using AR and VR technologies.**

5.4.3 Rehabilitation & Therapy in the Metaverse

- **VR Physical Therapy:** Stroke patients use VR exercises to **regain motor skills**.
- **Cognitive Therapy:** Alzheimer's patients experience **memory-enhancing**

simulations.

- **Pain Management:** VR environments help reduce **pain perception** for chronic

illness patients.
   Example:

- **Cedars-Sinai Hospital uses VR therapy** to help patients with **chronic pain management**.

5.5 Challenges of Metaverse Adoption

Despite its potential, the integration of the Metaverse into business, education, and healthcare comes with challenges:

5.5.1 Cost and Accessibility

- VR and AR hardware is still expensive, making it **inaccessible to many users**.
- Solution: **Cheaper VR devices and cloud-based access**.

5.5.2 Data Privacy and Security Risks

- Users' **biometric data, personal health records, and financial transactions** could be vulnerable.
- Solution: **Blockchain-based security and decentralized identity systems**.

5.5.3 Regulatory Uncertainty

- Governments have **no clear regulations** on Metaverse property rights and data privacy.
- Solution: **Standardized global Metaverse laws**.

5.6 Future Prospects of Metaverse in Business, Education, and Healthcare

The Metaverse will continue to expand into these sectors with advancements in:

- **AI and Automation:** Smart AI assistants will enhance virtual workplaces,

classrooms, and medical consultations.

- **5G and Cloud Computing:** Faster internet will allow **real-time, high-quality virtual**

interactions.

- **Full-Sensory VR Experiences:** Future VR headsets will include **touch, smell, and**

motion feedback.

5.7 Conclusion

The Metaverse is transforming **business, education, and healthcare** by making **work, learning, and medical treatment more immersive, efficient, and accessible**. While challenges like **cost, privacy, and regulation** exist, continuous advancements in **AI, blockchain, and VR technology** will drive widespread adoption.

In the next chapter, we will explore **"Social Interaction, Entertainment, and Culture in the Metaverse"**, discussing how digital identities, virtual relationships, and online communities are shaping the future of human interaction.

6

Social Interaction, Entertainment, and Culture in the Metaverse

6.1 Introduction

The Metaverse is redefining how people **interact, socialize, entertain themselves, and express culture** in digital spaces. Unlike traditional social media platforms, which offer limited engagement, the Metaverse creates **immersive, real-time interactions** that mimic real-world social dynamics. From **virtual friendships and relationships to concerts, digital fashion, and cultural movements**, the Metaverse is shaping the future of human connection.

This chapter explores the evolution of **social interaction, digital communities, entertainment, and cultural expression** within the Metaverse, along with its challenges and future trends.

6.2 Social Interaction in the Metaverse

The Metaverse allows users to interact through **avatars, voice chat, gestures, and shared experiences**, making virtual interactions more **lifelike and engaging**.

6.2.1 Digital Identities and Avatars

- **Customized Digital Avatars:** Users can create **hyper-realistic or stylized avatars**, reflecting their real-world appearance or fantasy personas.
-
- **NFT-Based Identities:** Some platforms offer **NFT avatars**, allowing users to own and trade unique digital identities.
-
- **Cross-Platform Avatars:** Future Metaverse systems aim to enable **one avatar across multiple virtual worlds**.

Example:

- **Meta's Horizon Worlds** allows users to create **full-body avatars** that interact using hand tracking and facial expressions.
- **Ready Player Me** offers **cross-platform avatars** that can be used in multiple Metaverse applications.

6.2.2 Virtual Friendships and Relationships

- **Social VR Spaces:** People can meet, chat, and build relationships in **virtual lounges, cafes, and social hubs**.
- **Metaverse Dating:** VR dating apps allow users to **go on virtual dates** with customized settings.

- **Digital Communities:** Online groups with shared interests gather in the Metaverse to engage in discussions, events, and activities.

Example:

- **VRChat and AltspaceVR** host thousands of users daily who form **friendships and even romantic relationships** in virtual reality.

6.2.3 Work and Social Networking in the Metaverse

- **Virtual Co-Working Spaces:** Professionals network and collaborate in immersive Metaverse office spaces.
- **Metaverse Conferences & Events:** Business leaders, entrepreneurs, and influencers attend **virtual summits and networking events**.
- **Branding and Personal Identity:** People showcase their **Metaverse personas for career and social purposes**.

Example:

- **LinkedIn is exploring Metaverse networking**, where users could **attend job fairs and interviews in VR**.

6.3 Entertainment in the Metaverse

The Metaverse is revolutionizing **gaming, music, sports, and movie experiences**, turning them into **interactive, shared social activities**.

6.3.1 Metaverse Gaming & Play-to-Earn Economies

- **Immersive VR Gaming:** Players engage in fully immersive worlds with **real-time movement, touch, and sound interactions**.
- **Play-to-Earn (P2E) Models:** Gamers earn cryptocurrency and NFTs that have real-world value.
- **Community-Driven Gaming:** Users **build, trade, and monetize** virtual gaming assets.

Example:

- **Axie Infinity and Decentraland** allow players to earn cryptocurrency by participating in Metaverse activities.

6.3.2 Virtual Concerts and Music Festivals

- **Metaverse Concerts:** Artists perform in **virtual stadiums** with interactive features.
- **NFT Music Ownership:** Fans buy and trade music NFTs, allowing direct artist-to-fan transactions.
- **VR Dance Clubs and Festivals:** Users attend DJ sets and clubbing events in virtual spaces.

Example:

- **Travis Scott's Fortnite Concert (2020)** was attended by over **12 million players** in a groundbreaking virtual event.
- **Ariana Grande's Metaverse tour** in Fortnite featured **interactive environments and avatar-powered choreography**.

6.3.3 Virtual Sports and eSports

- **Metaverse Stadiums:** Sports fans watch live matches in **virtual stadiums with interactive features**.
- **eSports Growth:** Competitive gaming tournaments attract **millions of viewers and participants**.
- **Digital Sports Gear & Collectibles:** Users buy NFT-based **sports memorabilia and virtual jerseys**.

Example:

- **NBA Top Shot sells NFT basketball highlights**, allowing fans to own and trade moments in sports history.
- **The Metaverse Olympics concept** is being explored for virtual reality-based global sports events.

6.3.4 Virtual Movie Theaters and Cinematic Experiences

- **VR Movie Theaters:** Users watch films with friends in **Metaverse cinemas** with realistic seating and sound.
- **Interactive Films:** Viewers participate in **choose-your-own-adventure storytelling** experiences.
- **Metaverse Film Festivals:** Independent filmmakers showcase movies in **virtual film festivals**.

Example:

- **Venice Film Festival launched a VR section**, allowing audiences to experience movies in an immersive setting.

6.4 Cultural Expression in the Metaverse

The Metaverse is enabling new forms of **cultural representation, digital fashion, and art movements**.

6.4.1 Digital Fashion and Wearable NFTs

- **Virtual Clothing & Accessories:** Users buy and wear **NFT-based outfits, shoes, and accessories**.
- **Fashion Metaverse Shows:** Luxury brands host **virtual fashion weeks** with digital-only collections.
- **Wear-to-Earn Models:** Users earn cryptocurrency by showcasing branded digital fashion.

Example:

- **Gucci, Louis Vuitton, and Balenciaga** have launched **NFT fashion collections** in Metaverse platforms.

6.4.2 Virtual Art Galleries and NFT Art Movement

- **Decentralized Art Galleries:** Artists showcase and sell NFT-based artwork in **Metaverse exhibitions**.
- **AI-Generated Art:** AI-powered tools create unique Metaverse art.
- **Ownership & Royalties:** Blockchain technology ensures **artists get paid for secondary sales**.

Example:

- **Beeple's $69 million NFT sale** proved that digital art could be as

valuable as physical art.
- **The Museum of Crypto Art (MOCA)** in Decentraland features top NFT artworks.

6.4.3 Cultural and Religious Communities in the Metaverse

- **Virtual Religious Gatherings:** Churches, temples, and mosques hold **services and spiritual meetups in VR.**
- **Cultural Heritage Sites:** Users explore **3D reconstructions of historical landmarks.**
- **Language & Cultural Exchange:** People from different countries **interact and learn about each other's traditions.**

Example:

- **A VR replica of Mecca** allows Muslims to experience a virtual Hajj pilgrimage.

6.5 Challenges of Social and Cultural Life in the Metaverse

While the Metaverse offers **new social, entertainment, and cultural opportunities**, it also presents **ethical and technological challenges.**

6.5.1 Digital Identity Theft & Privacy Issues

- **Fake avatars and stolen identities** pose security risks.
- Solution: **Decentralized identity verification** using blockchain.

6.5.2 Digital Divide & Accessibility

- Not everyone can afford **VR headsets or high-speed internet**, limiting participation.
- Solution: **More affordable hardware and cloud-based Metaverse experiences**.

6.5.3 Ethical & Behavioral Issues

- **Cyberbullying, harassment, and misinformation** can be amplified in virtual spaces.
- Solution: **AI moderation, strict policies, and digital well-being initiatives**.

6.6 Future of Social Interaction, Entertainment, and Culture in the Metaverse

The next decade will see advancements in:

- **Holographic Avatars:** AI-powered avatars that **mimic human behavior in real time**.
- **Metaverse AI Companions:** Digital assistants and AI-driven personalities for social interaction.
- **Digital Twin Cities:** Entire real-world cities will have **Metaverse counterparts for tourism and social experiences**.

6.7 Conclusion

The Metaverse is **reshaping social interaction, entertainment, and culture**, creating new ways for people to connect, express themselves, and engage with media. As technology advances, the future of the Metaverse will offer **even more immersive, inclusive, and**

interactive experiences, merging **virtual and real-world cultures** like never before.

In the next chapter, we will explore **"The Economy of the Metaverse: Digital Assets, Cryptocurrencies, and NFT Marketplaces"**, analyzing how financial ecosystems are evolving in virtual worlds.

7

The Economy of the Metaverse – Digital Assets, Cryptocurrencies, and NFT Marketplaces

7.1 Introduction

The Metaverse is not just a virtual space for socializing and entertainment—it is also a rapidly evolving **digital economy** with real-world financial implications. Businesses, individuals, and investors are actively participating in **virtual commerce, cryptocurrency transactions, and NFT marketplaces** to generate wealth and create new financial models.

This chapter explores the **fundamental aspects of the Metaverse economy**, including **digital assets, cryptocurrencies, decentralized finance (DeFi), NFT marketplaces, and the challenges and opportunities in this new financial landscape**.

7.2 The Metaverse Economy: An Overview

The Metaverse economy is powered by **digital ownership, blockchain technology, and decentralized transactions**, enabling users to earn, spend, and invest in virtual goods and services.

7.2.1 Characteristics of the Metaverse Economy

Decentralization: Most Metaverse economies are built on blockchain, reducing reliance on traditional banks.

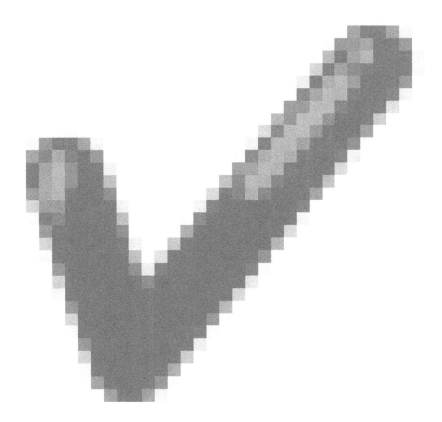

Digital Ownership: Users can own **virtual land, fashion, collectibles, and gaming assets** through NFTs.

Cryptocurrency Integration: Virtual economies use **tokens and stablecoins** for transactions.

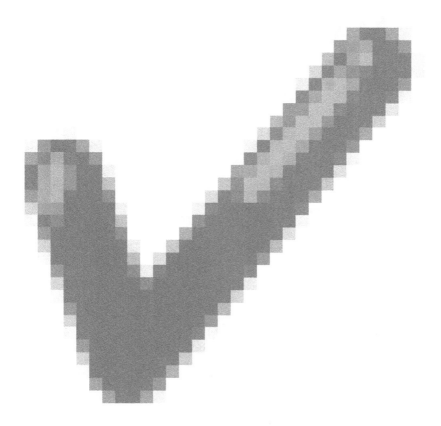

Interoperability: Digital assets can be **transferred between different Metaverse platforms**.

 Example:

- **Decentraland and The Sandbox** allow users to buy virtual land, build businesses, and trade digital assets using blockchain technology.

7.2.2 Blockchain and Smart Contracts in the Metaverse

Blockchain ensures security and transparency for all Metaverse transactions.

Smart contracts automate digital agreements, ensuring trust and reducing fraud.

Decentralized identity systems protect user data and enable secure transactions.

Example:

- **Ethereum and Solana** are widely used for Metaverse smart contracts and NFT transactions.

7.3 Cryptocurrencies in the Metaverse

Cryptocurrencies are the primary medium of exchange in the Metaverse, powering virtual economies and enabling peer-to-peer transactions.

7.3.1 Types of Cryptocurrencies in the Metaverse

Metaverse Tokens: Used within specific platforms (e.g., **MANA for Decentraland, SAND for The Sandbox**).

Stablecoins: Pegged to real-world assets for price stability (e.g., **USDT, USDC**).

Interoperable Cryptos: Bitcoin and Ethereum can be used across multiple Metaverse platforms.

    Example:

- **Axie Infinity's AXS and SLP tokens** allow players to earn cryptocurrency by participating in Metaverse-based gaming.

7.3.2 Decentralized Finance (DeFi) in the Metaverse

Metaverse Banking: Virtual banks offer loans, savings, and investments in cryptocurrency.

Yield Farming & Staking: Users earn passive income by **lending and staking digital assets**.

Decentralized Exchanges (DEXs): Users trade Metaverse tokens on platforms like **Uniswap and PancakeSwap**.

Example:

- **JPMorgan opened a virtual banking lounge in Decentraland**, signaling the rise of Metaverse financial services.

7.4 NFT Marketplaces and Digital Ownership

NFTs (Non-Fungible Tokens) play a crucial role in the Metaverse economy, representing **unique digital assets** such as virtual land, fashion, artwork, and collectibles.

7.4.1 What Are NFTs?

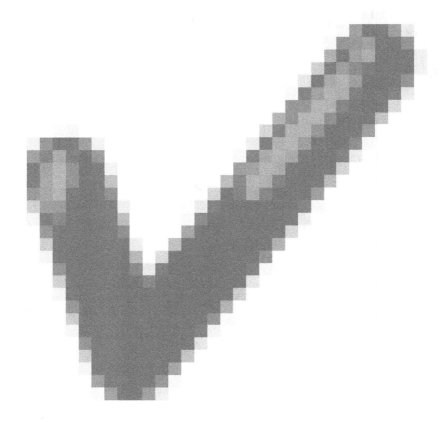

Unique & Verifiable: NFTs prove **ownership of digital goods** using blockchain.

Interoperable: They can be **traded across multiple Metaverse platforms**.

Smart Contract Integration: Ensures **automatic royalties** for creators.

7.4.2 Virtual Land and Real Estate in the Metaverse

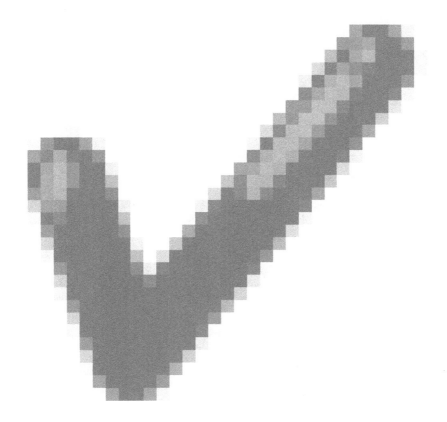

Metaverse Land Sales: Users buy, sell, and rent virtual land on platforms like **Decentraland and The Sandbox**.

Virtual Real Estate Development: Landowners build **digital businesses, concert venues, and NFT galleries**.

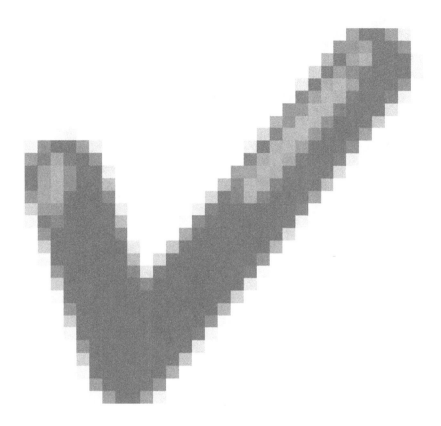

Rental & Advertising: Businesses lease **billboards and event spaces** in the Metaverse.

Example:

- In **2021, a plot of land in Decentraland sold for $2.4 million**, highlighting the growing demand for virtual real estate.

7.4.3 Digital Fashion and Wearable NFTs

NFT Fashion Items: Users buy digital clothing, shoes, and accessories for their avatars.

Luxury Brands in the Metaverse: Companies like **Gucci, Nike, and Balenciaga** sell NFT-based fashion collections.

Wear-to-Earn Models: Users earn rewards for showcasing digital fashion in virtual worlds.

Example:

- **Nike's RTFKT Studios sells limited-edition virtual sneakers as NFTs.**

7.4.4 Virtual Art and Music Ownership

NFT Art Galleries: Artists display and sell digital artwork in Metaverse museums.

Music NFTs: Musicians sell exclusive tracks as NFTs, bypassing record labels.

Metaverse Performances: Fans buy NFT-based concert tickets for exclusive events.

Example:

- **Beeple's NFT artwork sold for $69 million**, proving the value of digital art.

7.5 Income Generation and Jobs in the Metaverse

The Metaverse is creating **new career opportunities and revenue streams**, allowing people to earn a living through virtual work.

7.5.1 Play-to-Earn (P2E) and Work-to-Earn Models

Gaming for Income: Players earn crypto through gameplay in **Axie Infinity, Decentraland, and The Sandbox**.

Freelancing in the Metaverse: Users offer services like **3D design, coding, and marketing**.

AI-Powered Jobs: Virtual assistants and AI-driven NPCs (non-playable characters) generate revenue.

Example:

- **The Philippines saw a rise in play-to-earn workers**, where thousands made money through **Axie Infinity**.

7.5.2 Virtual Entrepreneurship and E-Commerce

Metaverse Stores: Entrepreneurs set up digital shops selling **NFTs, digital services, and avatar accessories**.

Event Planning & Hosting: Users organize **Metaverse weddings, concerts, and business conferences**.

Affiliate Marketing & Sponsorships: Influencers earn through brand partnerships in virtual worlds.

Example:

- **Influencers on platforms like Roblox and VRChat earn from brand sponsorships.**

7.6 Challenges in the Metaverse Economy

Despite its rapid growth, the Metaverse economy faces several hurdles that need to be addressed.

7.6.1 Market Volatility and Financial Risks

- Cryptocurrencies and NFTs **fluctuate in value**, creating financial risks.
- Solution: **Stablecoin adoption and risk management education.**

7.6.2 Cybersecurity and Fraud

- **Hacks, scams, and identity theft** are major concerns in decentralized economies.
- Solution: **Enhanced blockchain security and AI-powered fraud detection.**

7.6.3 Regulatory and Legal Uncertainty

- Governments are still **developing regulations** for Metaverse taxation and financial compliance.
- Solution: **Global legal frameworks for digital asset ownership and transactions.**

7.7 The Future of the Metaverse Economy

As technology advances, the Metaverse economy will continue to evolve, offering:

Interoperable Metaverse Currencies: A unified digital currency for all virtual worlds.

AI-Powered Virtual Assistants: AI-driven financial advisors and trading bots in the Metaverse.

Decentralized Autonomous Organizations (DAOs): Community-governed digital economies.

Metaverse Stock Markets: Virtual trading platforms for investing in digital businesses.

7.8 Conclusion

The Metaverse economy is revolutionizing **digital ownership, finance, and employment**, creating a **new era of decentralized commerce**. While challenges like **volatility, security, and regulation** remain, continued innovation in **blockchain, AI, and smart**

contracts will drive further adoption.

In the next chapter, we will explore **"The Ethical and Legal Implications of the Metaverse"**, discussing issues like **privacy, security, digital rights, and governance** in virtual worlds.

8

The Ethical and Legal Implications of the Metaverse

8.1 Introduction

As the Metaverse expands, it introduces complex ethical and legal challenges. Issues such as **data privacy, digital identity, virtual crime, content moderation, and governance** must be addressed to ensure a fair and secure virtual environment. The decentralized nature of the Metaverse creates **new regulatory dilemmas**, forcing governments, companies, and users to rethink legal frameworks and ethical guidelines.

This chapter explores the **ethical considerations, legal challenges, and proposed solutions** that will shape the future of law and morality in the Metaverse.

8.2 Ethical Concerns in the Metaverse

The Metaverse is designed for **human interaction, business, and entertainment**, but ethical concerns arise regarding **privacy, security, inclusivity, and psychological well-being**.

8.2.1 Privacy and Data Security

User Surveillance: Companies collect vast amounts of biometric, behavioral, and personal data.

Data Ownership: Users often lack control over how their **VR movements, conversations, and transactions** are used.

Targeted Advertising: AI-driven ads exploit **user preferences, emotions, and browsing history**.
   Example:

- **Meta's VR headsets track eye movement**, raising concerns about how gaze data could be monetized.

Potential Solutions:

- **Decentralized identity systems** to give users ownership over personal data.
- **Zero-knowledge proofs** to enable private transactions without exposing user identity.

8.2.2 Digital Identity and Consent

Identity Theft & Deepfakes: AI-generated avatars and voice mimicking can **impersonate real people**.

Informed Consent: Users may unknowingly agree to **excessive tracking or content manipulation**.

Anonymity vs. Accountability: While anonymity protects privacy, it can also enable **harassment and fraud**.
   Example:

• **A journalist in VRChat reported incidents of identity impersonation and harassment**, demonstrating the risks of unregulated avatars.

Potential Solutions:

- **Blockchain-based identity verification** to authenticate real users.
- **AI-powered moderation tools** to detect and remove fake identities.

8.2.3 Digital Well-Being and Mental Health

Addiction and Overuse: Immersive experiences can lead to **escapism, social withdrawal, and digital addiction**.

Psychological Effects of Virtual Harassment: Users may experience trauma from in-game abuse, cyberbullying, and discrimination.

Blurring of Reality and Virtuality: Some individuals may struggle to **distinguish real life from the Metaverse**, leading to dissociation. **Example:**

- **A woman in Meta's Horizon Worlds reported experiencing virtual harassment**, highlighting the emotional impact of VR abuse.

Potential Solutions:

- **Ethical Metaverse design**, including **built-in session limits and mental health support**.
- **AI-driven content moderation** to reduce harmful interactions.

8.2.4 Economic and Labor Ethics

Exploitation of Metaverse Workers: Some P2E (play-to-earn) economies rely on **low-wage digital labor**.

Monopolization of Virtual Economies: A few corporations may dominate Metaverse markets.

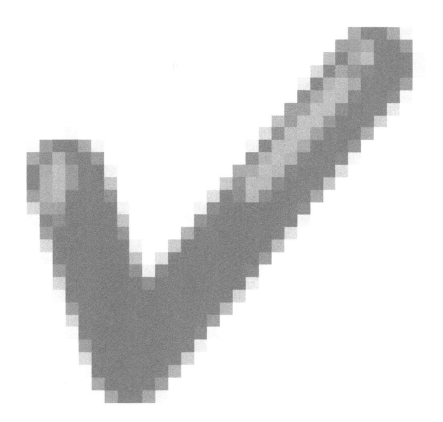

Taxation and Wealth Distribution: Governments struggle to **tax virtual assets and crypto earnings fairly**.

Example:

- **Axie Infinity's economic crash** led to financial losses for low-income players in the Philippines.

Potential Solutions:

- **Fair labor laws for digital work** in Metaverse economies.
- **Decentralized financial governance** to ensure equal economic participation.

8.3 Legal Challenges in the Metaverse

The Metaverse raises fundamental **legal questions about digital ownership, cybercrime, governance, and liability**.

8.3.1 Intellectual Property Rights in the Metaverse

Who Owns Virtual Creations? Artists, game developers, and brands create **digital assets, but ownership laws remain unclear**.

NFT Copyright Infringement: Some users steal art and tokenize it as NFTs without **creator consent**.

Brand Imitation in Virtual Worlds: Companies face challenges **protecting their trademarks** in digital spaces.

Example:

- **Hermès sued an NFT artist for creating "MetaBirkins,"** a virtual handbag collection that resembled their real-world products.

Potential Solutions:

- **Smart contract enforcement** to protect artists and creators.
- **International copyright laws** that apply to virtual content.

8.3.2 Virtual Crime and Law Enforcement

Cyber Harassment and Assault: Virtual harassment, threats, and stalking are difficult to police.

Financial Crimes & Fraud: Money laundering, Ponzi schemes, and crypto fraud are rising in virtual economies.

Hacking & Identity Theft: Malicious actors steal **Metaverse assets, NFTs, and personal data**.
Example:

- **A hacker exploited a flaw in OpenSea's smart contract, stealing $1.7 million worth of NFTs.**

Potential Solutions:

- **AI-driven cybercrime detection** to monitor Metaverse activity.
- **International cybersecurity laws** for digital asset protection.

8.3.3 Governance and Jurisdiction Issues

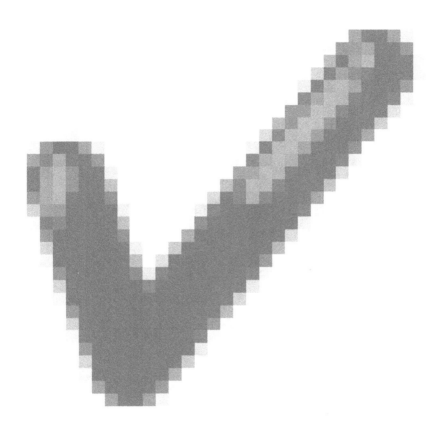

Who Governs the Metaverse? Unlike real-world countries, **no universal government controls digital worlds**.

Cross-Border Legal Conflicts: If a crime occurs in the Metaverse, which country's law applies?

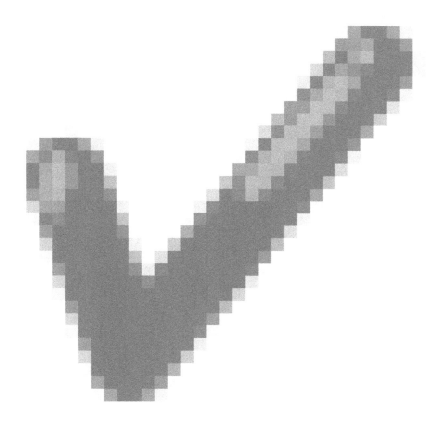

Regulating DAOs (Decentralized Autonomous Organizations):
These self-governing groups **lack legal recognition** in most countries.
Example:

- **Facebook's proposed Diem (Libra) cryptocurrency failed due to regulatory pushback,** showing the difficulty of digital governance.

Potential Solutions:

- **Metaverse-specific legal frameworks** that define jurisdictional authority.
- **Public-private collaborations** for ethical Metaverse governance.

8.4 Case Studies: Legal Precedents in the Metaverse

Several high-profile cases have tested the legal boundaries of the Metaverse.

8.4.1 The Roblox Lawsuit (2022)

Issue: Roblox faced lawsuits over **unlicensed music in its Metaverse**.

Outcome: The company **paid millions in settlements** to music labels, setting a precedent for digital copyright enforcement.

8.4.2 Second Life and Virtual Property Disputes

Issue: Users in Second Life sued after their **virtual land was deleted** without compensation.

Outcome: Courts ruled that **digital property can hold real-world legal value**.

8.4.3 The DAO Hack (2016)

Issue: A hacker exploited a flaw in an Ethereum-based **Decentralized Autonomous Organization (DAO)**.

Outcome: Ethereum developers "forked" the blockchain, reversing the hack, but raising ethical questions about blockchain immutability.

8.5 Future of Ethics and Law in the Metaverse

As Metaverse technology advances, the **legal and ethical landscape will continue to evolve**. Potential developments include:

AI-Powered Digital Courts: Smart contracts and AI judges resolving Metaverse disputes.

Global Digital Constitutions: Establishing universal Metaverse rights and responsibilities.

Tokenized Legal Systems: Using blockchain for **self-regulating governance**.

Privacy-Focused Metaverse Platforms: Decentralized networks with **enhanced user control**.

8.6 Conclusion

The Metaverse presents **groundbreaking opportunities** but also **unprecedented ethical and legal challenges**. From privacy concerns to cybercrime, digital property disputes, and AI governance, addressing these issues requires a **collaborative approach between governments, tech companies, and users**.

In the next chapter, we will explore **"The Future of the Metaverse: Opportunities and Challenges,"** examining how the Metaverse will shape **education, healthcare, AI, and global economies** in the coming decades.

9

The Future of the Metaverse – Opportunities and Challenges

9.1 Introduction

The Metaverse is still in its early stages, but its potential to **transform industries, economies, and social interactions** is undeniable. From **education and healthcare** to **AI-driven virtual worlds and decentralized economies**, the future of the Metaverse promises groundbreaking advancements. However, it also comes with **challenges related to scalability, governance, inclusivity, and ethics**.

This chapter explores the **opportunities and obstacles** that will define the evolution of the Metaverse, shaping its long-term impact on society and technology.

9.2 Opportunities in the Metaverse

The Metaverse presents **transformative possibilities** across various sectors, creating **new business models, innovative learning environments, and revolutionary healthcare solutions**.

9.2.1 The Future of Work and Virtual Offices

Decentralized Workspaces: Employees can work remotely in **VR-powered offices**, collaborating with colleagues worldwide.

AI-Powered Work Environments: AI-driven virtual assistants enhance productivity.

Metaverse Job Creation: New careers in **virtual real estate, digital marketing, and 3D design** will emerge.
  Example:

- **Microsoft's Mesh platform** integrates holographic meetings, enabling remote teams to work in immersive environments.

Potential Impact:

- Companies will invest in **Metaverse workplaces**, reducing physical office expenses.
- AI will **automate routine tasks**, allowing employees to focus on creativity and innovation.

9.2.2 Education and Learning in the Metaverse

Immersive Classrooms: Students can attend **3D virtual lectures, historical reconstructions, and interactive science experiments**.

Personalized AI Tutors: AI-driven virtual teachers will offer **customized learning experiences**.

Global Access to Education: Students from remote areas can access **high-quality virtual education.**
   Example:

- **Harvard and Stanford** are experimenting with **VR-based learning programs** to enhance student engagement.

Potential Impact:

- Traditional education will shift toward **Metaverse-based interactive learning**.
- **Skill-based training in VR** will replace many **traditional classroom methods**.

9.2.3 Healthcare and Therapy in the Metaverse

VR-Powered Medical Training: Surgeons and doctors can practice **complex procedures in virtual simulations**.

Mental Health Support: Patients can attend **therapy sessions in immersive VR environments**.

Remote Patient Consultations: Virtual clinics will make **healthcare more accessible** worldwide.

Example:

- **Johns Hopkins University successfully performed a surgery using AR and VR-assisted guidance.**

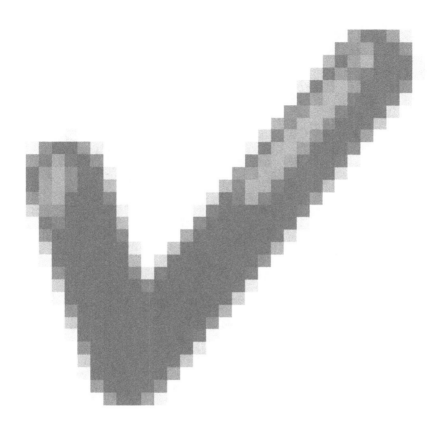

Potential Impact:

- AI-powered virtual doctors will **analyze patient data and offer real-time diagnosis**.
- **Metaverse therapy sessions** will improve mental health care, especially for those in remote areas.

9.2.4 AI and Automation in the Metaverse

AI-Generated Worlds: The Metaverse will feature AI-powered **dynamic environments** that evolve based on user interactions.

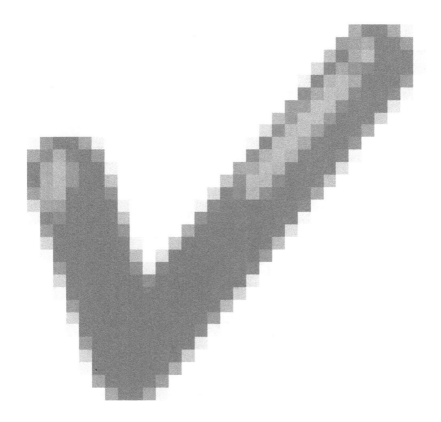

Intelligent NPCs (Non-Player Characters): AI-driven avatars will **assist, teach, and interact with users** in real time.

Smart Contracts for Automation: Decentralized **AI-powered financial and legal services** will operate autonomously.

Example:

- **ChatGPT-powered avatars** will act as virtual customer support agents and educators.

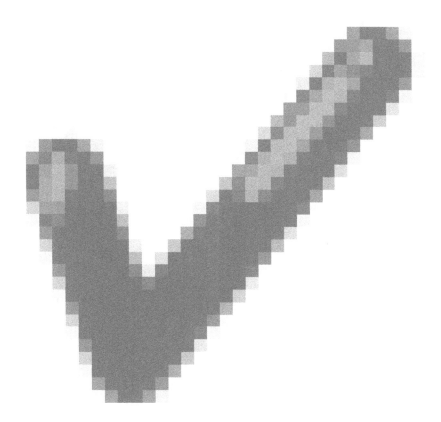

Potential Impact:

- AI will **enhance immersive storytelling**, making virtual experiences feel more realistic.
- Businesses will use **AI-driven avatars for marketing, consulting, and personal assistance**.

9.2.5 Metaverse for Social Impact and Inclusivity

Accessible Virtual Spaces: The Metaverse can be **designed for disabled individuals**, enabling **better social integration**.

Global Connectivity: People from different cultures can interact in **shared digital spaces**, promoting inclusivity.

Philanthropy and Social Change: Charities can host **virtual fundraising events** in the Metaverse.
   Example:

 • **UNICEF is exploring the Metaverse to provide educational resources for children in underprivileged communities.**

Potential Impact:

- The Metaverse will **bridge social and economic gaps**, creating **equal opportunities for all**.
- **Digital activism and humanitarian efforts** will expand in the virtual space.

9.3 Challenges Facing the Metaverse

Despite its potential, the Metaverse faces **significant challenges that could hinder its growth and adoption**.

9.3.1 Scalability and Technological Limitations

High Computing Power Requirements: The Metaverse demands **powerful hardware and high-speed internet** for seamless experiences.

Latency and Performance Issues: Current **network infrastructure struggles** to support real-time interactions.

Storage and Bandwidth Constraints: Large-scale virtual environments require **massive data processing capabilities**.

　Example:

- **Meta's Horizon Worlds has faced technical glitches and performance issues**, limiting user engagement.

Potential Solutions:

- **5G and next-gen cloud computing** will enhance connectivity and reduce latency.
- **Quantum computing advancements** will improve real-time rendering of digital worlds.

9.3.2 Security and Privacy Risks

Hacking and Cybercrime: Virtual wallets, NFTs, and digital identities are vulnerable to theft.

Data Privacy Concerns: Companies can **track user behavior, facial expressions, and biometric data**.

Content Moderation Challenges: Ensuring **safe and ethical inter-actions** in a decentralized space is difficult.

Example:

- **Hackers stole $600 million from Axie Infinity's blockchain network**, highlighting security vulnerabilities.

Potential Solutions:

- **Decentralized identity verification** to prevent identity theft.
- **AI-powered fraud detection** to monitor and block cybercriminal activity.

9.3.3 Ethical and Legal Issues

Who Regulates the Metaverse? The lack of **centralized governance** creates legal confusion.

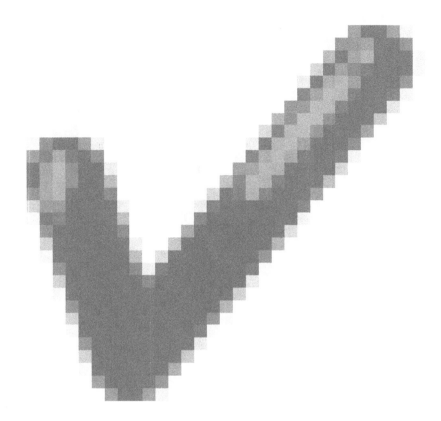

Virtual Property Rights: Digital land and assets lack **clear ownership protections**.

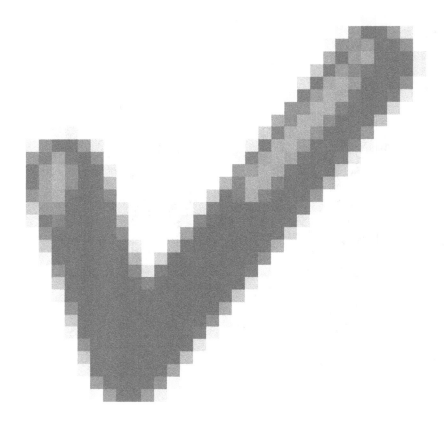

AI Bias and Ethical Dilemmas: AI-driven experiences may reinforce **biases in virtual interactions**.

Example:

- **Meta has struggled to implement effective moderation policies in its virtual spaces**, leading to safety concerns.

Potential Solutions:

- **International regulatory frameworks** to establish clear Metaverse laws.
- **Transparent AI policies** to prevent algorithmic bias.

9.3.4 Environmental Impact of the Metaverse

High Energy Consumption: Blockchain-based Metaverse platforms **consume large amounts of electricity**.

E-Waste from VR Devices: Frequent upgrades of **VR headsets and hardware contribute to electronic waste**.

Sustainability Concerns: Current Metaverse models **lack eco-friendly design principles**.
   Example:

- **Bitcoin mining and NFT transactions have been criticized for their environmental impact.**

Potential Solutions:

- **Green blockchain technology** like Ethereum's transition to Proof-of-Stake (PoS).
- **Energy-efficient VR and AR hardware** to reduce carbon footprints.

9.4 The Road Ahead: What's Next for the Metaverse?

The Metaverse will continue evolving, driven by **technological innovation, regulatory developments, and user adoption.**

Hyper-Realistic Virtual Experiences: Advancements in **haptic feedback, brain-computer interfaces (BCIs), and holographic technology**.

AI-Powered Virtual Companions: Personalized digital assistants that **learn and adapt to user preferences**.

Mass Adoption of Web3 Technologies: Decentralized platforms will make **virtual ownership mainstream**.

Interoperable Metaverse Ecosystems: Users will **seamlessly move assets and identities** across different platforms.

9.5 Conclusion

The Metaverse represents the next **evolution of digital interaction**, offering immense potential for **business, education, healthcare, and entertainment**. However, **scalability, security, regulation, and**

ethical concerns must be addressed to ensure its sustainable growth.

As we move toward a **fully immersive digital future**, collaboration between **governments, corporations, and users** will be crucial in shaping an inclusive, ethical, and secure Metaverse.

10

Conclusion and Final Thoughts

[1]10.1 Introduction

The Metaverse represents a paradigm shift in how humans interact, work, play, and conduct business in a digital-first world. Over the past chapters, we have explored its **technological foundations, economic potential, social implications, and ethical challenges**. Now, it is time to step back and examine the **big picture**—where the Metaverse stands today, what hurdles it must overcome, and what its future might hold.

---

[1] **A Final Thought: The Future is Unwritten**

The Metaverse is not just about **technology**; it is about **people**. It is about how we **choose to build, engage with, and regulate** the next iteration of the digital world. Unlike previous technological revolutions that unfolded with limited foresight, **we now have the chance to shape the Metaverse consciously and ethically**.

As you read this book, I encourage you to **think critically, ask questions, and imagine possibilities**. The Metaverse is not an inevitable destination—it is **a canvas upon which we can create the future we want to see**.

The journey into the Metaverse has already begun. Let's ensure that it is a journey **toward innovation, inclusion, and empowerment**—not just for the tech elite, but for all of humanity.

163

This chapter provides a **comprehensive conclusion** to our discussion by summarizing key findings, analyzing future possibilities, and offering recommendations for navigating the Metaverse responsibly.

10.2 Summary of Key Insights

Throughout this book, we have examined the **Metaverse from multiple perspectives**. Below is a recap of the essential takeaways:

10.2.1 The Evolution of the Metaverse

From Early Virtual Worlds to Web3: The Metaverse has evolved from **text-based virtual environments like MUDs to VR-powered worlds and blockchain-based economies**.

Technological Foundations: The Metaverse relies on **VR, AR, blockchain, AI, and cloud computing**.

Web3 and Decentralization: Unlike earlier digital spaces, the modern Metaverse is increasingly driven by **user ownership and decentralized governance**.

10.2.2 Economic and Business Potential

Virtual Real Estate: Digital land is now **a multi-billion-dollar market**, attracting investors and businesses.

Metaverse-Based Jobs: Professions like **virtual architects, NFT designers, and AI trainers** are emerging.

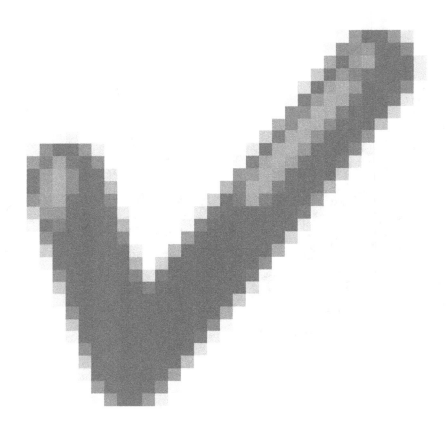

Brand Expansion into Digital Worlds: Companies like **Nike, Gucci, and Disney** have launched Metaverse experiences.

10.2.3 Social and Psychological Implications

Digital Identity and Self-Expression: Users are adopting **avatars and virtual personas** that reflect their desired identity.

Mental Health and Well-Being: The Metaverse offers **both benefits and risks** related to mental health, including **VR therapy and digital addiction concerns**.

Privacy and Ethical Issues: The **monetization of user data, AI surveillance, and virtual crime** remain significant concerns.

10.2.4 Legal and Ethical Challenges

Intellectual Property and Digital Ownership: Who owns **NFTs, digital land, and AI-generated content** remains a legal gray area.

Cybersecurity Risks: Virtual asset theft, fraud, and **identity imper-sonation** pose real threats.

Global Regulation of the Metaverse: Governments struggle to enforce laws in a **borderless, decentralized digital world**.

10.2.5 The Future Potential of the Metaverse

AI-Generated Virtual Worlds: The rise of **AI-powered Metaverse experiences** will make digital spaces more dynamic.

Healthcare and Education Transformation: VR surgery training, mental health therapy, and immersive classrooms will redefine these sectors.

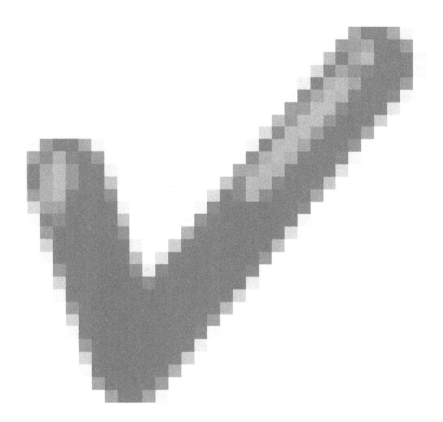

The Rise of Interoperability: The ability to move **digital assets, avatars, and identities** across multiple Metaverse platforms will enhance user experiences.

10.3 Challenges That Could Slow the Growth of the Metaverse

Despite its promise, the Metaverse is still far from achieving mainstream adoption. Several key challenges could delay or complicate its development.

10.3.1 Technological Limitations

Hardware Accessibility: VR/AR devices are still expensive, limiting adoption.

Energy Consumption: Blockchain-powered Metaverse ecosystems require enormous computing resources.

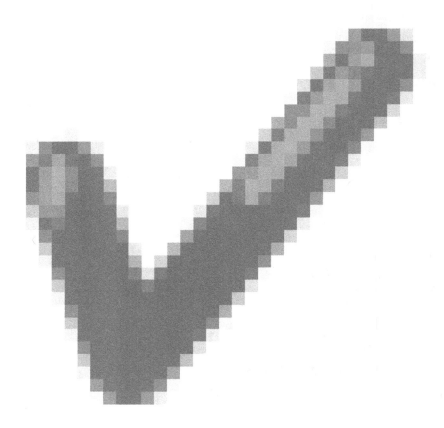

Latency and Bandwidth Issues: Seamless Metaverse experiences demand **high-speed internet, 5G, and edge computing advancements**.

Potential Solutions:

- **Affordable VR Headsets**: Companies like Meta, Apple, and Sony are working on **cheaper, more efficient VR/AR devices**.
- **Green Blockchain Solutions**: Transitioning to **energy-efficient proof-of-stake systems** will reduce environmental impact.

10.3.2 Ethical and Legal Concerns

Privacy Invasion: AI-driven data collection could **track eye movements, brain activity, and biometric patterns**.

Virtual Crime & Abuse: **Harassment, scams, and AI deepfake identity theft** are rising concerns.

Legal Uncertainty: The Metaverse lacks clear regulations regarding **taxation, copyright, and digital property disputes**.

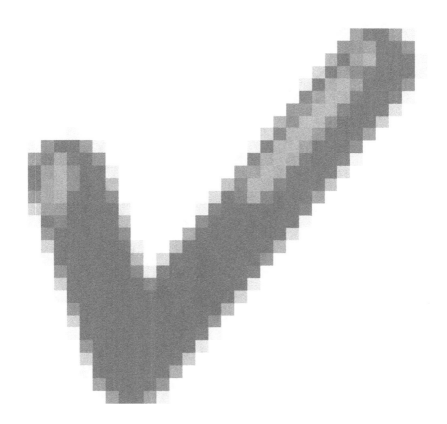

Potential Solutions:

- **Ethical AI Development**: Transparent AI policies and **bias-free algorithm training**.
- **Metaverse-Specific Legislation**: Governments must work with **tech companies and blockchain communities** to create fair digital laws.

10.3.3 Digital Divide and Accessibility Issues

Who Gets to Participate? The Metaverse risks **excluding marginal-ized communities** due to cost barriers.

Cultural and Linguistic Barriers: Not all digital spaces **support diverse languages and accessibility features**.

Neurodiversity & Disabilities: Virtual spaces are not always designed **with inclusivity in mind**.

Potential Solutions:

- **Publicly Funded Metaverse Access**: Governments and NGOs could provide **Metaverse education and free entry points for underprivileged communities**.
- **Universal Design Principles**: Ensuring Metaverse platforms cater to **disabled users, neurodivergent individuals, and different language speakers**.

10.4 The Long-Term Vision for the Metaverse

Where does the Metaverse go from here? Several possible futures exist, depending on how society, technology, and business evolve.

10.4.1 A Fully Integrated Digital Society

The Metaverse as an Extension of Reality: A future where **virtual and physical realities seamlessly blend**.

Smart Cities with Metaverse Integration: AR-powered navigation, virtual tourism, and AI-driven public services.

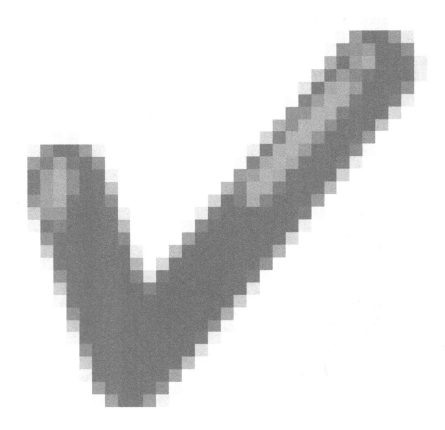

Brain-Computer Interfaces (BCIs): Directly linking human cognition with digital spaces, **eliminating the need for screens and controllers**.

10.4.2 A Decentralized and User-Owned Metaverse

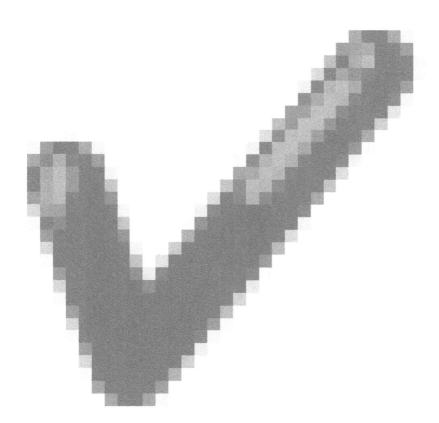

DAO Governance: Community-led decision-making through **decentralized autonomous organizations (DAOs)**.

No Single Corporate Owner: A Metaverse that **resists monopolization by tech giants**.

Web3-Powered Ownership: Users **own their data, digital assets, and experiences**, rather than corporations.

10.4.3 A Fragmented Metaverse Controlled by Big Tech

Walled Gardens: Competing tech companies **create separate, in-compatible digital worlds** (e.g., Meta's Horizon Worlds vs. Apple's Vision Pro ecosystem).

Data Centralization: AI-driven tracking, targeted advertising, and **corporate control over user behavior**.

Pay-to-Play Economy: Access to premium Metaverse experiences **requires expensive subscriptions and in-game purchases**.

10.4.4 A Dystopian Future? Risks of an Overpowered Metaverse

Surveillance Capitalism: Governments and corporations **monitor every aspect of digital life**.

AI-Controlled Social Systems: AI algorithms dictate **which content is seen, which jobs are available, and how people interact**.

Loss of Real-World Human Connection: Society **becomes too reliant on virtual interactions**, reducing in-person communication.

How to Avoid This?

- **Advocacy for Digital Rights**: Global efforts to **protect user privacy and freedom**.
- **Open-Source Metaverse Development**: Encouraging **transparent, community-driven innovation**.

10.5 Final Thoughts: The Role of Individuals, Businesses, and Governments

The Metaverse's future is **not set in stone**—it will be shaped by the choices made by **users, companies, and policymakers**.

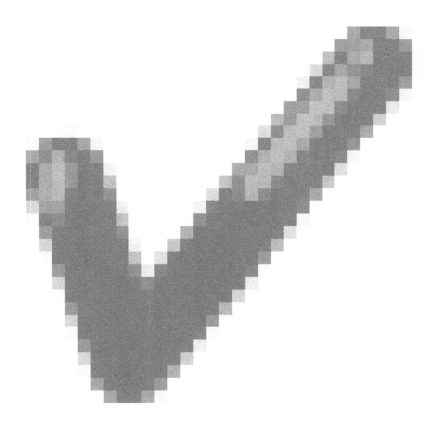

For Individuals:

- Educate yourself about **Metaverse ethics, privacy, and digital ownership**.
- Participate in **open-source and decentralized Metaverse communities**.

For Businesses:

- Develop **ethical Metaverse products** with a focus on user well-being.
- Avoid monopolistic practices and **prioritize interoperability**.

For Governments:

- Establish **global regulatory standards** for digital assets and virtual economies.

- Protect user privacy and **combat digital exploitation**.

10.6 Conclusion

The Metaverse represents **both an opportunity and a challenge**—a new digital frontier that could **redefine human existence**. If developed responsibly, it has the potential to **enhance creativity, improve education, and create new economic opportunities**. However, if mismanaged, it could lead to **privacy violations, social inequality, and corporate monopolization**.

The future of the Metaverse is **in our hands**—how we shape it will determine whether it becomes a **utopia or a dystopia**.

10.7 A Call to Action

The Metaverse is not just a **technological phenomenon**—it is a **societal transformation**. As we stand at the brink of this new digital frontier, it is crucial that individuals, businesses, and governments take an **active role** in shaping its development.

10.7.1 For Individuals

Educate Yourself: Stay informed about Metaverse advancements, blockchain technologies, and virtual economies. Follow research, attend webinars, and engage with Metaverse communities.

Practice Digital Responsibility: Protect your privacy by understanding data policies, securing digital assets, and being mindful of AI-driven interactions.

Advocate for Ethical Innovation: Support companies that prioritize **decentralization, inclusivity, and sustainability** in their Metaverse projects.

Engage with Open Metaverse Projects: Join open-source initiatives and decentralized platforms that promote **user-driven governance and creativity**.

10.7.2 For Businesses

Develop Ethical Metaverse Solutions: Companies must **prioritize transparency, user control, and security** in their virtual platforms.

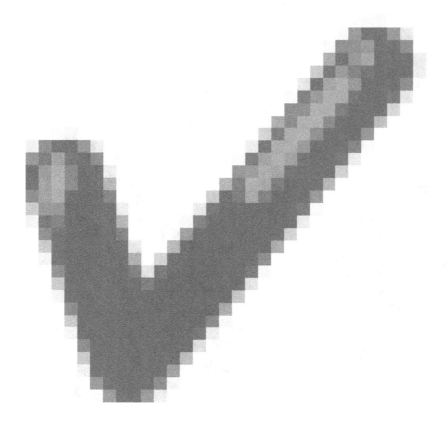

Support Interoperability: The future Metaverse should allow users to transfer assets, avatars, and data seamlessly across multiple platforms.

Create Inclusive Digital Spaces: Design Metaverse environments that cater to **diverse cultural backgrounds, abilities, and economic classes**.

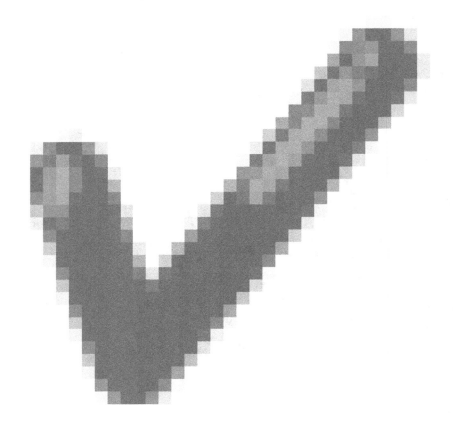

Invest in Digital Literacy and Workforce Training: The transition to Metaverse-based work environments requires new skills—businesses should **offer education and training programs**.

10.7.3 For Governments and Policymakers

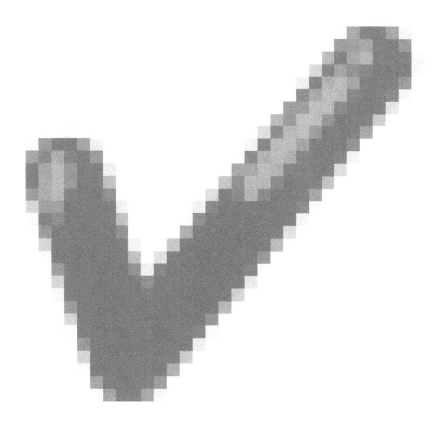

Establish Global Digital Governance: Governments should **collaborate on regulatory frameworks** that ensure security, digital rights, and ethical AI deployment.

Protect Digital Privacy: Implement data protection laws that prevent **corporate overreach and AI surveillance abuses**.

Encourage Innovation and Competition: Avoid monopolization by **supporting decentralized platforms and fair economic models**.

Address Cybersecurity Threats: Invest in **AI-driven fraud detection, Metaverse law enforcement, and digital forensics** to combat cybercrime.

The **Metaverse is ours to shape**, but it requires **active participation, critical thinking, and ethical leadership** to ensure that it benefits all of humanity rather than a select few.

10.8 Future Research Directions

While significant progress has been made, many **unanswered questions** remain about the Metaverse's long-term impact. Future research should explore the following key areas:

10.8.1 AI and Ethical Automation in the Metaverse

- How do we ensure that AI-driven avatars, assistants, and NPCs **do not reinforce biases** or manipulate user behavior?
- What are the risks of **AI-powered Metaverse governance**, and how can we design **human-centered regulatory models**?
- How can we **create AI that enhances creativity and learning** rather than replacing human interaction?

10.8.2 Metaverse Governance and Law

- How should **intellectual property laws** evolve to accommodate **NFTs, virtual assets, and AI-generated content**?
- What **international legal frameworks** are needed to regulate decentralized economies?
- How do we ensure **ethical content moderation and digital human rights** in immersive virtual spaces?

10.8.3 Social and Psychological Effects

- What long-term effects will **extended Metaverse immersion** have on human cognition, attention spans, and social skills?
- How do we design **healthy digital environments** that promote **mental well-being instead of digital addiction**?
- Can virtual reality therapy **truly replace traditional mental**

health treatments, and how do we ensure accessibility?

10.8.4 Sustainability and Environmental Impact

- How can we **reduce the carbon footprint** of blockchain-based Metaverse economies?
- What innovations in **energy-efficient VR/AR hardware** can make the Metaverse more sustainable?
- Can decentralized AI and **green blockchain protocols** balance economic growth with environmental responsibility?

Research in these areas will be **crucial in determining whether the Metaverse remains a force for good** or becomes an unregulated, high-risk digital landscape.

10.9 Final Reflections

The **Metaverse is no longer science fiction**—it is a rapidly evolving reality. We are witnessing the **birth of a digital civilization**, where human interaction, economy, and culture are **reshaped by virtual and augmented experiences**.

However, we must **ask ourselves difficult questions**:

Are we building a Metaverse **for profit or for people**?

Will it empower individuals **or become another tool for corporate and government surveillance**?

Can it foster **meaningful human connections**, or will it further isolate us in digital bubbles?

The **answer lies in our collective actions**. The choices we make today—how we design, regulate, and engage with the Metaverse—will determine its **impact on future generations**.

As we step into this **uncharted digital frontier**, we must remember that **technology should serve humanity, not the other way around**. The Metaverse, at its best, should be an **inclusive, immersive, and ethical space** that enhances creativity, learning, and economic opportunity for all.

The future of the Metaverse is **in our hands**—how we shape it will determine whether it becomes a **utopia or a dystopia**.

11

References

Here is a list of citations and references with hyperlinks to authoritative sources on the Metaverse:

General Understanding of the Metaverse

1. **Ball, M. (2022).** *The Metaverse: And How it Will Revolutionize Everything.* W.W. Norton & Company.

- https://www.amazon.com/Metaverse-How-Will-Revolutionize-Everything/dp/1324092033

1. **Dionisio, J.D.N., Burns III, W.G., & Gilbert, R. (2013).** *3D Virtual Worlds and the Metaverse: Current Status and Future Possibilities.* ACM Computing Surveys, 45(3).

- https://dl.acm.org/doi/10.1145/2480741.2480753

Technologies Behind the Metaverse

1. **Stephenson, N. (1992).** *Snow Crash.* Bantam Books. *(Fictional origin of the term "Metaverse")*

   • https://www.penguinrandomhouse.com/books/17183/snow-crash-by-neal-stephenson/

1. **Meta (2021).** *The Future of Connection in the Metaverse.* Meta Platforms, Inc.

   • https://about.fb.com/news/2021/10/founders-letter/

1. **Rosenberg, L. (2022).** *The AI and VR Convergence: The Dawn of Intelligent Virtual Worlds.* IEEE Spectrum.

   • https://spectrum.ieee.org/artificial-intelligence-and-virtual-reality

Metaverse Economy and NFTs

1. **Coindesk (2022).** *A Guide to NFTs and the Metaverse Economy.*

   • https://www.coindesk.com/learn/what-is-the-metaverse

1. **Zuckerberg, M. (2021).** *Building the Metaverse Economy.* Meta (Facebook).

   • https://about.fb.com/news/2021/10/building-the-metaverse/

1. **Grayscale Research (2021).** *The Metaverse: Web 3.0 Virtual Cloud*

Economies.

- https://grayscale.com/insights/the-metaverse-web-3-0-virtual-cloud-economies/

Social, Psychological, and Ethical Implications

1. **IEEE (2022).** *Ethical Challenges of AI-Driven Metaverse Interactions.*

- https://www.ieee.org/ethics-in-metaverse.html

1. **World Economic Forum (2023).** *Governance and Regulation of the Metaverse.*

- https://www.weforum.org/reports/metaverse-governance

Future of the Metaverse

1. **PwC (2023).** *The Metaverse and the Future of Work.*

- https://www.pwc.com/gx/en/issues/metaverse/the-metaverse-and-the-future-of-work.html

1. **Gartner (2022).** *Metaverse: Hype Cycle and Long-Term Impact.*

- https://www.gartner.com/en/newsroom/press-releases/2022-07-06-gartner-says-25-percent-of-people-will-spend-at-least-one-hour-per-day-in-the-metaverse-by-2026

www.ingramcontent.com/pod-product-compliance
Lightning Source LLC
LaVergne TN
LVHW051445050326
832903LV00030BD/3250